I Can Be Anything!

I CAN BE A RACE CAR DRIVER

By Nancy Greenwood

Please visit our website, www.garethstevens.com. For a free color catalog of all our high-quality books, call toll free 1-800-542-2595 or fax 1-877-542-2596.

Cataloging-in-Publication Data
Names: Greenwood, Nancy.
Title: I can be a race car driver / Nancy Greenwood.
Description: New York : Gareth Stevens Publishing, 2021. | Series: I can be anything! | Includes index.
Identifiers: ISBN 9781538255667 (pbk.) | ISBN 9781538255681 (library bound) | ISBN 9781538255674 (6 pack)
Subjects: LCSH: Automobile racing drivers–Juvenile literature.
Classification: LCC GV1029.13 G737 2021 | DDC 796.72–dc23

First Edition

Published in 2021 by
Gareth Stevens Publishing
111 East 14th Street, Suite 349
New York, NY 10003

Editor: Kate Mikoley
Designer: Laura Bowen

Photo credits: Cover, p. 1 (kid) Cool_photo/Shutterstock.com; cover, pp.1 (background), 7, 9, 11, 13, 24 (track) Action Sports Photography/Shutterstock.com; p. 5 Nomad_Soul/Shutterstock.com; pp. 15, 24 (helmet) TOSP/Shutterstock.com; p. 17 Jared C. Tilton/Stringer/Getty Images North America/Getty Images; p. 19 Doug James/Shutterstock.com; pp. 21, 24 (flag) Feng Yu/Shutterstock.com; p. 23 Icon Sports Wire/Contributor/Icon Sportswire/Getty Images.

Printed in the United States of America

CPSIA compliance information: Batch #CS20GS: For further information contact Gareth Stevens, New York, New York at 1-800-542-2595.

Contents

This is Joe.
He's a race car driver!

Joe's car is a stock car.
It is very strong.

6
6

The race is on a track.
It is an oval.

NASCAR Sprint

Cars go around the track many times. These are laps.

Sprint
CUP SERIES
CHEVROLET
24

Race cars go fast!
Sometimes they crash.

10
22

Drivers wear helmets.

Fans come to watch.
They sit in the stands.

A fence keeps fans safe.

A checkered flag
means there's a winner!
The race is over.

I can be a
race car driver.
So can you!

Words to Know

flag

helmet

track

Index

SIMPLE MACHINES ALL AROUND US

SCREWS

At Work

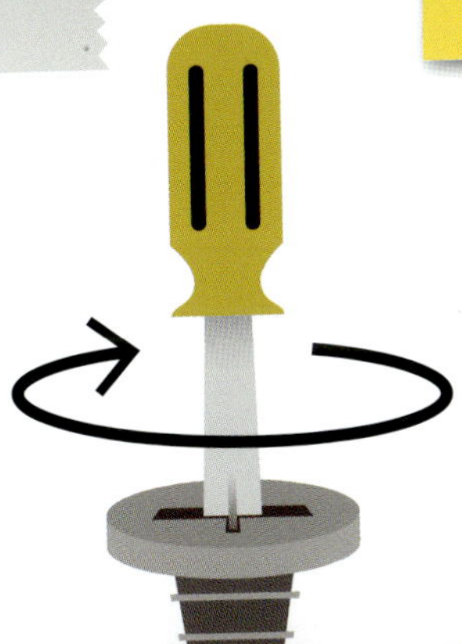

By Maggie S. Wesley

DISCOVER!

Please visit our website, www.enslow.com. For a free color catalog of all our high-quality books, call toll free 1-800-398-2504 or fax 1-877-980-4454.

Library of Congress Cataloging-in-Publication Data

Names: Wesley, Maggie S., author.
Title: Screws at work / Maggie S. Wesley.
Description: New York : Enslow Publishing, 2022. | Series: Simple machines all around us | Includes bibliographical references and index.
Identifiers: LCCN 2020028575 (print) | LCCN 2020028576 (ebook) | ISBN 9781978520929 (library binding) | ISBN 9781978520905 (paperback) | ISBN 9781978520912 (set) | ISBN 9781978520936 (ebook)
Subjects: LCSH: Screws–Juvenile literature.
Classification: LCC TJ1338 .W46 2022 (print) | LCC TJ1338 (ebook) | DDC 621.8/82–dc23
LC record available at https://lccn.loc.gov/2020028575
LC ebook record available at https://lccn.loc.gov/2020028576

Published in 2022 by
Enslow Publishing
101 West 23rd Street, Suite #240
New York, NY 10011

Designer: Katelyn E. Reynolds
Editor: Kristen Nelson

Photo credits: Cover, pp. 1 Nasky/Shutterstock.com; cover, pp. 1–24 (background and typeface) Reytr/Shutterstock.com; cover, pp. 1–24 (paper) jannoon028/Shutterstock.com; cover, pp. 1–24 (note sticker) Kindlena/Shutterstock.com; p 5 Ryouchin/ DigitalVision/ Getty Images; p. 6 Robert Lowdon/Moment/Getty Images; p. 7 Aerotoons/ DigitalVision Vectors/Getty Images; p. 8 Designua/ Shutterstock.com; p. 9 Andrea Nissotti / EyeEm/Getty Images; p. 11 George Diebold/ The Image Bank / Getty Images Plus; p. 12 Capelle.r/Moment/Getty Images; p. 13 Wibofoto/E+/Getty Images; p. 13 (inset) lucentius/ iStock / Getty Images Plus; p. 15 PavelRodimov/ iStock / Getty Images Plus; p. 17 Simon Battensby/ Photographer's Choice / Getty Images Plus; p. 19 Audtakorn Sutarmjam / EyeEm/Getty Images; p. 21 (lightbulb) Aleksander Kaczmarek/ iStock / Getty Images Plus; p. 21 (drill bit) naruedom/ iStock / Getty Images Plus; p. 21 (bottle and cap) TPopova/ iStock / Getty Images Plus; p. 21 (faucet and hose) photka/ iStock / Getty Images Plus.

Portions of this work were originally authored by Gillian Houghton Gosman and published as *Screws in Action*. All new material this edition authored by Maggie S. Wesley.

Printed in the United States of America

CPSIA compliance information: Batch #CSENS22: For further information contact Enslow Publishing, New York, New York, at 1-800-398-2504.

Contents

Boldface words appear in Words to Know.

What Is a Screw?

Simple machines have few or no moving parts. They make work easier to do. A screw is a simple machine. It is commonly used to hold things in place. The other kinds of simple machines are levers, pulleys, inclined planes, wheels and axles, and wedges.

SCREWS COME IN MANY SHAPES AND SIZES.

Screw Parts

A wood screw is a short metal bar shaped like a **cylinder**. The cylinder comes to a point. The length of the screw is called its shaft. At one end, there is a flat or rounded head. The head has a specially shaped slot to fit a screwdriver's tip.

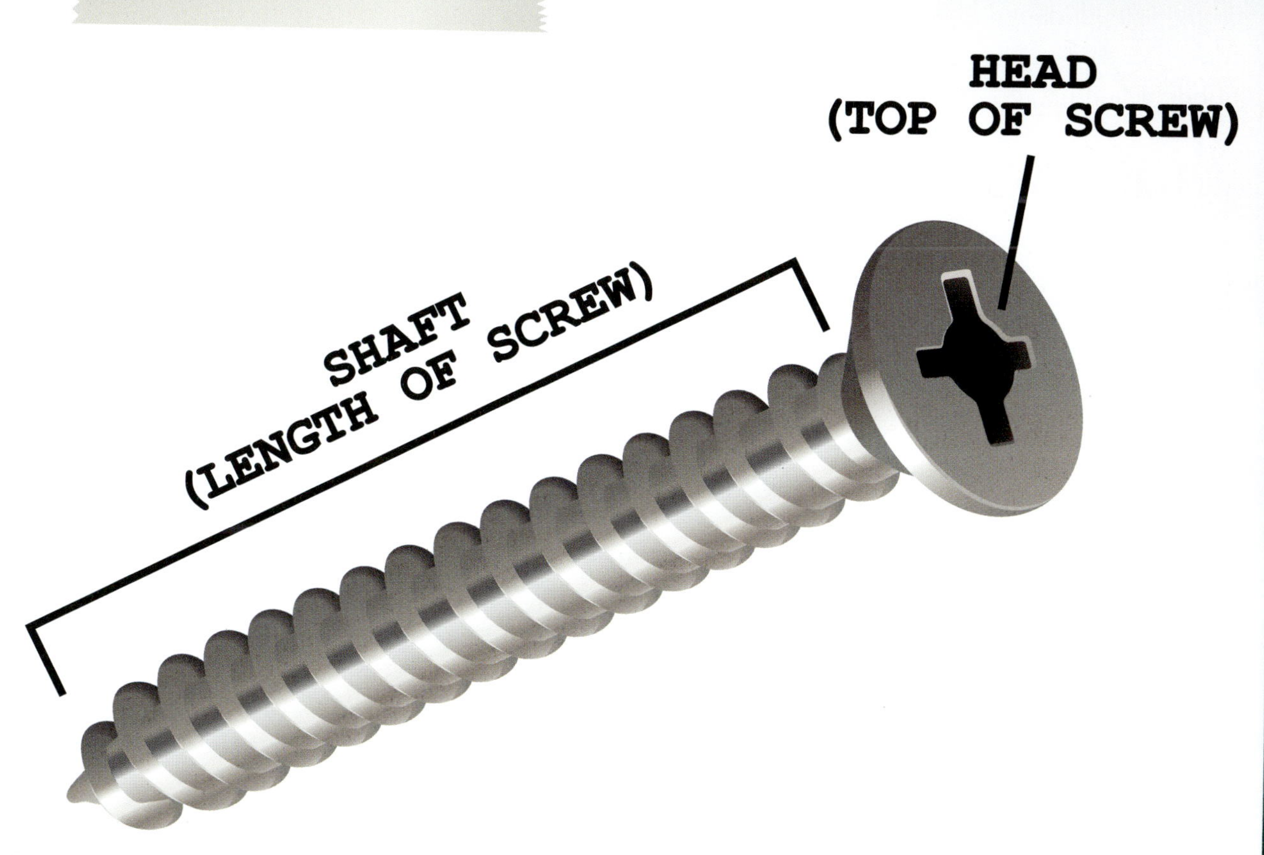
HEAD
(TOP OF SCREW)
SHAFT
(LENGTH OF SCREW)

A screw's shaft has a metal **ridge** that wraps around it. This is the screw's thread. The thread is an inclined plane wrapped around the cylinder of the screw. As a **force** turns the screw, the inclined plane of the thread meets the **material** around it.

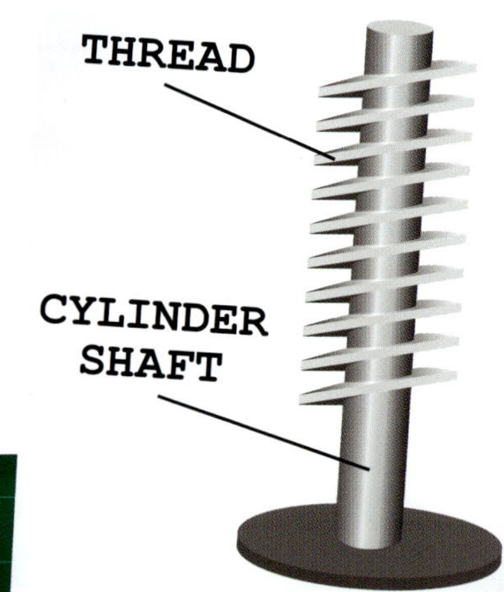

AN INCLINED PLANE IS A FLAT SURFACE **ANGLED** SO ONE END IS HIGHER THAN THE OTHER. IT MAKES MOVING LOADS EASIER.

Why Screws Work Well

Different types of screws may have smaller or greater spacing between the threads of the screw. The distance between threads is called the pitch. The closer together the threads are, the greater the mechanical advantage of the screw. This means it takes less effort to turn the screw into a material.

SCREWS CAN BE THICK OR THIN.

Drills or screwdrivers are used to drive screws into and pull screws out of a material. The tip of the drill or screwdriver is placed in the slot at the top of the screw. It then twists the head of the screw. The threads of the screw cut into the material.

SCREWS HOLD SOMETHING IN PLACE BETTER THAN NAILS BECAUSE OF THE THREADS CUTTING INTO THE MATERIAL.

Other Screws

A screw's thread may also meet an **interlocking** thread in the material around it. For example, the thread on the inside of a bottle cap is meant to interlock with the thread around the mouth of the bottle. This holds the cap on the bottle.

IF THE TWO THREADS DO NOT MEET THE RIGHT WAY, THE SCREW WILL JAM, OR STOP.

A bolt is a special kind of screw used to hold things together. It has a flat end and a matching nut, or a ring of metal with interlocking threads. You are using the idea of the bolt and nut when you twist a lid onto a screw-top jar.

BOLT
NUT

PUTTING PRESSURE

Screws may be used to put **pressure** on something. For example, a clamp is a tool that may use the turning of a screw to tighten its arms. The more the screw is turned, the better the clamp can hold something in place. Screws can also be used to hold and lift something.

CLAMP

Find Screws Around You

Screws are at work all around you! They hold your bookshelf together and are used to hang pictures on the wall. Screws hold the lids on your pickle and jelly jars. Screws are an important simple machine to everyone! What other screws can you find in your home?

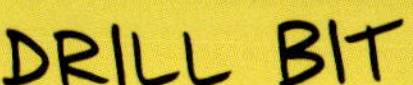

NOZZLE AND HOSE

Words to Know

angle To point something so that it's not flat.

cylinder An object shaped like a tube.

force A power or effect that can change the speed or direction of something.

interlocking Connecting two things together.

material Matter from which something is made.

pressure A force that pushes on something else.

ridge A raised area on the surface of something.

For More Information

Books

Blevins, Wiley. *Let's Find Screws.* North Mankato, MN: Pebble, 2021.

Crane, Cody. *Simple Machines.* North Mankato, MN: Children's Press, 2019.

Websites

Simple Machines Facts

www.coolkidfacts.com/simple-machines-facts/
Find out more examples of all kinds of simple machines here.

What Is a Simple Machine?

http://www.wonderopolis.org/wonder/what-is-a-simple-machine
Answer more of your questions about simple machines using this fun website.

Publisher's note to educators and parents: Our editors have carefully reviewed these websites to ensure that they are suitable for students. Many websites change frequently, however, and we cannot guarantee that a site's future contents will continue to meet our high standards of quality and educational value. Be advised that students should be closely supervised whenever they access the internet.

Index